102 FAVORITE PAINTINGS by
NORMAN ROCKWELL

Norman Rockwell in his living room in Stockbridge, Mass.

102 FAVORITE PAINTINGS by

Norman Rockwell

With an Introduction by

CHRISTOPHER FINCH

AN Artabras BOOK

CROWN PUBLISHERS, INC.   NEW YORK, N.Y.

On the JACKET:

The Artist
Commentary on page 64

Library of Congress Cataloging in Publication Data
Rockwell, Norman, 1894–
    102 favorite paintings.

    1. Rockwell, Norman, 1894–   I. Rockwell,
Norman, 1894–   50 famous Rockwell favorites.
1978. II. Finch, Christopher. III. Title.
ND237.R68F556   759.13   77-26251

ISBN 0–517–534487

CONTENTS

102 FAVORITE PAINTINGS by
NORMAN ROCKWELL

INTRODUCTION

by CHRISTOPHER FINCH

NORMAN ROCKWELL IS A MASTER OF THE ART OF ILLUSTRATION, an art that he helped transform as technical advances that occurred during his lifetime brought high-quality color reproduction to the newsstands of the world. It is almost impossible, however, to discuss him simply as an artist and innovator because, by some mysterious chemistry, the images he created have become part of the fabric of our popular culture. He held up a friendly mirror to the society he lived in, and Americans have looked into this glass and seen themselves as warm, decent, hard-working citizens of a country bountiful enough to accommodate their boundless optimism.

There are those who object that Rockwell's mirror is of the distorting variety, and this may be true; but it could be argued that exactly the same can be said of many of the masters of, for example, the Italian Renaissance. When Andrea Mantegna immortalized the Gonzaga family on the walls of the Ducal Palace in Mantua, he undoubtedly idealized his patrons, lending them a nobility that had as much to do with their aspirations as with the everyday realities of their existence. This is not to say that the Gonzagas' aspirations were unreal or absurd. They reflected the ideals of the day, and Mantegna had the ability to make these ideals a reality, if only in paint and plaster.

Norman Rockwell's patrons were the millions of Americans who subscribed to periodicals like *The Saturday Evening Post* or who bought them on the street corner, in drugstores and railroad stations. Their ideals were far removed from those that prevailed at the ducal court of Mantua during the latter half of the fifteenth century. Rockwell's patrons grew up with the Bill of Rights and a tradition of grass-roots democracy. They were nourished on Mark Twain, Horatio Alger and Will Rogers. Their heroic models were not taken from Virgil and Ovid; they were drawn from the ranks of their own contemporaries—men and women like Charles Lindbergh and Amelia Earhart, who seemed to represent both an adherence to traditional American values and the ability to confront the future without fear. It should be added that, while Rockwell's patrons welcomed the existence of these heroes, they did not see themselves as heroic except when heroism was forced upon them by circumstances. When this did occur, as during World War II, Rockwell rose to the occasion with works such as his version of "Rosie the Riveter," based on a pose from Michelangelo's Sistine Chapel ceiling, and his celebrated "The Four Freedoms"; but even at this time he was more at home with Willie Gillis, his everyman in uniform.

Ironically, Rockwell—in his own quiet way—became a hero of the American public. As Rockwell would be the first to point out, there is little of the conventionally heroic about him. A modest, retiring man, not given to grand gestures, he impressed himself on America's collective imagination by his stubborn adherence to the old values. His ability to relate these values to the events and circumstances of a rapidly changing world made him a special person—both hero and friend—to millions of his compatriots. Norman Rockwell provided a commodity that people could rely on. Throughout a long career he has given his patrons a sense of continuity.

His art itself has consistently been a fascinating blend of the old and the new. In one respect Rockwell has always been a thoroughgoing traditionalist, working at an easel in oils, watercolors and other tried-and-true mediums, yet he has had to remain conscious of the fact that his work is intended to be seen not as an original but as a reproduction. He does his work in a studio, but before it reaches the public it is processed by the camera and by modern, high-speed, four-color presses. An illustrator must, for example, be a master of scale. This cannot be achieved by merely increasing the size of the canvas. The commercial artist must work within the limitations of a given format. Most of Rockwell's *Saturday Evening Post* covers were painted on canvases several times larger than the magazine itself, and it was essential that he keep in mind how the image would work once it was reduced for the presses. This is a highly specialized skill. Reproduced in books, many of the masterpieces of the past lose much of their impact since they were conceived as paintings that would be seen in the original on a wall. The artist never had any reason to think about how they would appear on the printed page. For an illustrator, however, this is the primary consideration, and Rockwell's work actually gains in power when it is reduced to a magazine or book format. Rockwell is a skillful artist, in traditional terms, but beyond that he is one of the most inventive visual journalists of the twentieth century. His greatest talent has been for creating magazine covers that jump out from crowded news racks—an essentially modern skill. *The Saturday Evening Post,* for example, could automatically increase its print order by 250,000 copies when an issue had a cover by Rockwell.

There have, or course, been other artists who have mastered the same principles, but Rockwell has been unique in that he alone has managed to modify his skills, again and again, throughout a career that has spanned more than six decades. From the beginning he has managed to stay abreast of public taste, and his reputation rests not on a handful of masterpieces but on the accumulation of thousands of images that have impressed themselves on the minds of several generations of Americans.

Not all of these images are of equal quality. The masterpieces are there, sure enough, but just as important—given the character of Rockwell's career—is the fact of his astonishing consistency. The ability to produce high-quality work, month after month, year after year, decade after decade, is in itself an extraordinary gift. If we try to place ourselves in Rockwell's position we will see, I think, that he may well have gained as much satisfaction from some of his everyday assignments as from the more obvious triumphs. For him, small victories are just as significant as major breakthroughs, and finding a new twist to a traditional theme means just as much as the discovery of a new one. Imagine, for instance, having come up with an original idea for a Christmas cover every year for more than half a century.

Norman Rockwell created a world that, because of its traditional elements, seems familiar to all of us, yet is recognizably his and his alone. He is an American original who has left his mark not by effecting radical change but rather by giving old subjects his own, inimitable inflection. His career has been an ode to the ordinary, a triumph of common sense and understatement.

Home Duty

MAY 20, 1916

WHEN NORMAN ROCKWELL WAS A young illustrator, in his early twenties, Clyde Forsythe—a cartoonist with whom he shared a studio at the time—told him that if he wanted to make something of himself he should shoot for the stars. The higher Rockwell's aim, Forsythe argued, the more he was likely to achieve. Rockwell took this advice to heart. The top market for illustrators at that time was *The Saturday Evening Post*—a weekly that had already been in existence for well over one hundred years—and the young hopeful decided to try his luck where the competition would be stiffest.

He painted two covers and made a sketch for a third, then took the train to Philadelphia, where he presented his work to Walter Dower, who was then the *Post*'s art editor. Rockwell was left to wait impatiently while Dower studied the work. When the art editor reappeared it was to inform Rockwell that the magazine was prepared to buy both of the finished works, wanted him to develop the sketch for a third cover and was ready to commission three more. Rockwell and the *Post* would be associated for the next forty-seven years.

This *Post* cover, which appeared in May 1916, was Rockwell's first. There would be 323 more—an average of almost seven a year.

Not Tall Enough

JUNE 16, 1917

WHEN THIS COVER—ROCKWELL'S NINTH for the *Post*—appeared, the United States had just entered the Great War and Rockwell was himself about to join the armed services—the U.S. Navy to be precise—with the exalted rank of third-class varnisher and painter. This particular subject may have been suggested to him by the fact that he had been rejected by the Navy, at the time of his initial application, on the ground that he was eight pounds underweight.

It is typical of Rockwell's work of this period that he translates the realities of the adult world into a children's game. He is able to do this convincingly because he realizes that children take their world every bit as seriously as adults take their own. Rockwell never patronizes the children in his paintings, and this allows us to identify with them.

Rockwell attempted to have himself posted to Europe but was unable to conceal his status as a well-known illustrator and was kept in the United States, where he was assigned to the staff of the Navy publication *Afloat and Ashore*. At the same time he continued to contribute paintings and drawings to the *Post* and many other magazines.

Pardon Me!

JANUARY 26, 1918

THE CLOTHES SPORTED BY THESE YOUNG partygoers place them firmly in their period, but the situation Rockwell pictures here is one that he might just as easily have tackled in the Thirties or the Fifties. Rockwell had only recently graduated to the *Post* from magazines like *Boy's Life*, and it is noticeable in these early covers that he was much more comfortable dealing with young folks than with adults.

The composition is competent rather than inspired, and the entire weight of the painting is carried by characterization. A study of Rockwell's early work will, in fact, demonstrate conclusively that he was first and foremost a skillful storyteller. Only some time later did he become an original visual artist.

The Nation's Hero

FEBRUARY 22, 1919

IT IS INTERESTING TO CONTRAST this cover with Rockwell's *Homecoming GI* (Page 77) painted at the end of World War II. In this earlier example Rockwell gave us a totally conventional representation of the returning hero. The proud doughboy stands erect, his head held high, surrounded by admiring kids who are reliving his brave deed in their imagination. The red-headed GI in the later work is an entirely different concept. He may have been just as brave, but he seems bemused by the situation and almost dwarfed by his surroundings.

The doughboy of 1919 is idealized by the artist. The GI of 1945 is humanized, and this is the measure of Rockwell's growth as an illustrator during the intervening years.

Courting Couple at Midnight

MARCH 22, 1919

THIS IS A FINE EXAMPLE OF ROCKWELL'S early cover art. Both situation and characters are beautifully conceived and executed to answer the demands of the medium. As the pendulum swings and the cuckoo emerges from its ornate lodging, the dapper young man—his hair just lightly ruffled—gasps in amazement, realizing that time has flown (as it is apt to do in these situations). His beloved wears an expression that suggests her emotions have soared beyond the mundane dictates of the clock. She is living an eternal moment of romantic bliss. Whether or not the cuckoo will succeed in shattering her reverie is open to question, but promises made to her parents are clearly running through the young man's head.

There is nothing idealized or generalized about this couple. They are, without a doubt, real people—people you might see crossing the street or riding the bus, the young woman a trifle plump, her beau a neighborhood dandy, almost choked by his high, stiff collar. In this respect this is already a mature Rockwell work. It is also a particularly well-painted canvas. The two heads, the girl's dress and the cushion she leans against are all handled with a wonderful economy. Rockwell has always understood that hands can be almost as expressive as faces, and here his treatment of the young man's hands is especially effective.

Leapfrog

JUNE 28, 1919

THE COVERS THAT NORMAN ROCKWELL painted in the years immediately after World War I placed a great emphasis on a return to normalcy and traditional values and subject matter. It was some time before the editors of the *Post* encouraged him to take note of the fact that America was changing—and changing rapidly—though, interestingly, throughout this period many other *Post* contributors, such as F. Scott Fitzgerald, presented readers with graphic accounts of those changing times. Clearly, the editors made a sharp distinction between the cover art, which was designed to sell the magazine, and the editorial content, which was governed by more flexible standards.

Given the limitations that were placed upon him at the time, it's extraordinary that Rockwell was able to come up with so many lively compositions. The subject matter of this 1919 example, for instance, could hardly be more simple and straightforward, but Rockwell managed to pep it up by using a time-honored trick of the trade, making it seem that the leap-frogging boy is almost literally jumping off the page.

A Boy's Best Friend

AUGUST 9, 1919

AT THE AGE OF NINETEEN NORMAN ROCKWELL became the art editor of *Boy's Life*. He soon moved on to more exalted things, but he never forgot this beginning, and in that respect he may be compared with another stalwart of *The Saturday Evening Post,* P. G. Wodehouse, who started his career writing stories for British schoolboy magazines. The two can, in fact, be compared in many ways: Both sustained extraordinarily long careers by remaining faithful to the values that had first made them popular.

Rockwell has always felt particularly comfortable portraying the everyday adventures of pre-adolescent boys. He understands their simple pleasures and the predictable crises of their lives. Many of his early *Post* covers were rooted in the kind of material he had produced for *Boy's Life*. In this example a dog has stolen the pants of the youthful bather. Rockwell simply took the kind of situation he had been called on to illustrate dozens of times and made a lively cover from it.

This may seem an easy enough thing to have done, but we should not lose sight of the fact that it was rather bold of him to use this *Boy's Life* kind of material on the cover of something as prestigious as the *Post*. From our perspective this cover may seem rather old-fashioned. At the time it was painted it represented a breath of fresh air in the context in which it appeared.

Portrait in Snow

DECEMBER 20, 1919

WHEN NORMAN ROCKWELL BEGAN TO WORK for the *Post*, that weekly had a set cover style and Rockwell was expected to adhere to its conventions. Everything—from subject matter to the color range the artist could employ—was predetermined by either editorial policy or technical considerations. This example is Rockwell's first Christmas cover for the *Post*—it had taken him just three years to win this honor, an assignment given only to the magazine's top contributors—and he gave the editors exactly what they were looking for: a traditional snow scene and a confrontation of youth and age leavened with a touch of gentle humor.

At this point in his career his expertise consisted primarily in being able to work to the demands of an established formula. Before long, however, he would begin to introduce personal notes into his paintings, and by the late Twenties most of his covers were quite distinctive; they could have been painted by no one but Rockwell. But it was not until the early Forties that he perfected the idiom, full of documentary detail, that has made him so famous.

Through all this he was, of course, influenced by shifting editorial policy and by exposure to the work of other artists, but as he assimilated new ideas Rockwell somehow always managed to give them an original twist, making them his own property. A steady growth from the conventional to the unique has been the hallmark of his career.

Looking Out to Sea

1919

THIS EARLY OIL PAINTING gives us a glimpse of Norman Rockwell's traditional roots. In subject matter it foreshadows much of his later work, but it lacks the personal touch that he brought to his mature work. We can use this totally academic study as a standard against which to measure his eventual achievement. All of the technical skill is there already, but the artist has not yet found a personal viewpoint. The figures here are ciphers of youth and age. In his maturity he would have endowed the old man and the boy with more character, making them distinct individuals, through the trenchant details that are so telling in Rockwell's later work.

No Swimming

JUNE 4, 1921

IN THIS FAMOUS *Post* COVER from early in Rockwell's career, three boys discover that a "No Swimming" sign means exactly what it says. Throughout Rockwell's work, but especially in his early paintings, boys—and girls too for that matter—are no better than they ought to be. Like Tom Sawyer and Huck Finn, they have a knack for getting into any kind of mischief that happens to be placed at their disposal.

This example shows how well Rockwell had already mastered the demands of the magazine-cover format. Note how cleverly he uses the black box that was then an integral part of the *Post*'s cover layout. The fact that the boy on the left is vanishing at the edge of this framing device helps to add emphasis to their haste. The box is like a searchlight that has caught them in its beam. If only they could escape its confines they would, we are encouraged to feel, be able to outdistance their pursuer.

Sitting for a Portrait

JULY 9, 1921

IN THIS EARLY COVER, ROCKWELL has once again chosen to illustrate a moment in human affairs with which we can all identify.

This young man being photographed with his baby sister is in an early portrait studio where the photographer has placed the head of the young man against a clamp so that there will be no movement to blur the finished photograph. But there can be no reckoning with the very young especially when bright lights are being shone in her face and she is expected to perform the impossible: sit without moving.

This kind of baby portraiture went out with the studio itself but what we respond to these 50 years later is the impossibility of getting a baby to sit still. No doubt an inventive mother, or an imaginative photographer will come up with a solution, but for now we participate in the young man's frustrated embarrassment and the baby's unhappy situation.

Man Threading a Needle

APRIL 8, 1922

IT IS A MARK OF NORMAN ROCKWELL's enormous skill that he has been able to make powerful covers out of the simplest and most unlikely subject matter. This one, painted for the *Post* in 1922, shows nothing more exotic than a middle-aged man attempting to thread a needle preparatory to darning one of his socks, yet it is one of his most successful covers of that period.

The composition is strong because it is so simple, but it is the wealth of carefully observed detail that brings the painting to life. The man's features are a wonderful study in concentration, his tongue held firmly between teeth and lips and his nose pointing the way for the thread to go. His torso is rigid, and his hands—which seem much too big for this job—are pressed together so as to steady each other. He sits on a backless chair on which rest his pipe and his daily newspaper, the company of which he would undoubtedly prefer to the task in hand. His cat, ignored, brushes up against his trouser legs.

We are not told whether he is a bachelor or whether his wife is out of town on a visit. But we can see that he is a man who is concerned with his appearance, and we empathize with his predicament. If we study the painting closely we will also notice that when he finishes with the sock he will still not be quite ready to repair to the comforts of his newspaper and pipe. A button is missing from his vest.

Private Concert

FEBRUARY 3, 1923

THROUGHOUT HIS CAREER, NORMAN ROCKWELL has been fascinated by the subject of elderly men playing musical instruments. Of all the arts, music is the one most famous for producing child prodigies—whether composers like Mozart, or performers like Yehudi Menhuin—but Rockwell has chosen to portray it as something that can best be savored with the passage of time. Almost exactly a year before he painted this cover, he had painted another—for *Literary Digest*—which was a moving portrait of a grey-haired concert violinist. He would return to the theme time and time again, the series culminating in one of his greatest works, *Shuffleton's Barber Shop* (Page 101), painted for the *Post* more than quarter of a century later.

This 1923 cover is a modest but charming example of the genre. The old man is very happy to play for his granddaughter to dance but we can guess that he also plays for himself, just as the musicians in the backroom of Shuffleton's barber shop play for themselves. Perhaps what attracted Rockwell to this subject was that he felt a touch of envy for those artists who could savor the pleasures of art at no matter how humble a level.

Christmas Trio

DECEMBER 8, 1923

WHEN NORMAN ROCKWELL WAS A BOY, on the upper West Side of Manhattan, his father was given to reading out loud passages from the works of Charles Dickens after supper while the boy sketched the characters. This early exposure to the great nineteenth-century novelist seems to have had a profound effect on Rockwell's subsequent career. In one sense it is true to say that almost all of Rockwell's work can be seen as an extension of the Dickensian tradition. Rockwell has Dickens' flair for caricature and for inventing colorful and picturesque characters. He has the same gift of creating comedy out of everyday situations.

Early in his career Rockwell often painted period pieces that were quite blatantly Dickensian in inspiration. A case in point is this Christmas cover. The man at the left of the group might be Mr. Pickwick himself. The boy is clearly a cousin of Oliver Twist, and it is not difficult to imagine Scrooge confronting the Ghost of Christmas Past in any of the buildings that form the background to this composition.

During the time he was painting period pictures Rockwell built up a large wardrobe of costumes in which he would dress his models. This collection was lost when his studio was destroyed by fire in 1943, and after that he seldom attempted such subjects again.

Dining Out

THE HISTORY OF TRAMPS AND HOBOES in America—both the gentlemen of the road and the fraternity of the rails—is a fascinating one and one that has not been fully told. As the nation spread westward a whole subculture developed around the men—and a few women—who, for a variety of reasons, abandoned the comforts of home and took to the dirt roads or rode the narrow rails of freight trains, moving from one shantytown "jungle" to the next, piecing together a living as best they could. These people developed their own code of ethics and even evolved their own elaborate patois—coining many new words that eventually entered the mainstream of the language. The word "dingbat," for example, was originally a hobo term applied by that brotherhood to the lowliest of its own members, the bums who were barely able to look after themselves.

The golden age of the hobo was the first quarter of this century, and his culture was already in decline by the onset of the Depression, at which time it was finally swamped by the hundreds of thousands of men—from farm hands to professors—who were forced to take to the freights because of hard times. These newcomers found themselves in the jungles out of necessity rather than choice and lacked the inclination to take up the wandering life as a permanent vocation.

The life of the hobo was, in truth, often brutish and cruel, but it had its romantic side, and it was an independent existence. It was that romantic side of the hobo world that Rockwell painted in this 1924 cover. The picture is not without its ominous edge, however. Fall has arrived. The trees are shedding their leaves, and we realize that this old tramp will soon have to face the hardships of another bitter winter.

First Love

APRIL 24, 1926

PERHAPS THE MOST REMARKABLE THING about this cover is that it seems so completely informal. Rockwell takes one of the standard *Post* formulas of the period and handles it with such ease that one smiles as much at his casual skill as at the subject matter. The circle—in this case representing the setting sun—eclipsing a portion of the logo had become a conventional device by this time, but note how Rockwell sets it off center, thus emphasizing the fact that the girl is leaning on the boy. This seems to be the first instance of Rockwell posing his main characters with their backs to the viewer, a trick that must have seemed quite daring when this cover appeared. The fact is that we do not need to see the faces; their expressions could add little to what the couple's posture tells us.

An interesting aspect of this painting is that the two figures are treated quite naturalistically but *appear* to be caricatured because of the clothes they are wearing. The boy's high-waisted trousers and the girl's oversized shoes alter the proportions of their bodies and add pathos to the scene. Even the sagging bench contributes to the overall mood of the picture.

Doctor and Doll

MARCH 9, 1929

THE MEDICAL PROFESSION IS ALWAYS treated sympathetically in Norman Rockwell's work. His doctors make house calls, take the time to chat with patients and have bedside manners worthy of Lionel Barrymore.

This elderly general practitioner is shown drawing on several decades of experience to break the ice with a nervous child. We can tell that the child has just arrived at his office, for she is still wearing a scarf and mittens. Her face is clouded with apprehension, but the doctor does his best to set her mind at rest by entering her fantasy world and placing his stethoscope to her doll's chest.

This painting is a good example of what might be called Rockwell's "old master" style. Many of his covers of this period emphasized two-dimensional design rather than painterly values. Here he falls back on his academic background, and we can be sure that he did so with very good reason. It may be that he felt that this idiom would reflect the tastes and values of the doctor who, presumably, began his practice in the Victorian era.

At the Breakfast Table

AUGUST 23, 1930

ONE OF NORMAN ROCKWELL'S GIFTS is his ability to bring fresh life to subjects that have become hackneyed. The scene that he treats here is a hoary one. At the breakfast table a wife finds herself isolated from her husband, who has buried himself in his newspaper. It is one of the oldest situations in the book. Even in 1930, when this was painted, the average reader of the *Post* must have encountered dozens of variations on it.

Rockwell approaches the theme with what almost amounts to a sense of reverence. The joke speaks for itself, so he does not attempt to overstate it but instead addresses himself to the poignancy of the situation. What he does, in effect, is to take the joke seriously.

All of his sympathy is directed toward the wife. Her pose tells us a good deal about her feelings. She is pressed up against the table as if she longs for physical contact with her husband. Her face expresses resignation but not yet despair. This marriage, we feel, has only recently entered this phase.

It is left to us to decide where this breakfast scene will lead. It is perhaps worth noting, however, that it was painted at a point in Rockwell's life when he had recently been divorced by his first wife.

Home from Vacation

SEPTEMBER 13, 1930

ALTHOUGH THERE IS NOTHING PARTICULARLY clever or original about this 1930 painting for a *Post* cover, it is a fine example of a genre that Rockwell always handled with such skill that he eventually made it his own. The poses of the three figures tell us all that needs to be known about the subject, but there are many quiet embellishments—the escaping frog, the limp daisies, the deflated balloon—that add greatly to the success of the composition.

Had this cover been painted ten years later, Rockwell would probably have given this exhausted young family a more detailed setting, but in most respects this painting has all the elements that we associate with his maturity as an illustrator. We sense a total confidence in the way he has handled the subject. He knows exactly what must be done to make the situation believable, and he does it with a minimum of fuss.

Going Out

OCTOBER 21, 1933

BECAUSE OF NORMAN ROCKWELL'S preoccupation with the everyday aspects of the world, we do not generally think of him as being at home with silks and satins—gingham would seem to be more his speed—but his expertise in this area is clearly demonstrated in this *Post* cover dating from the first year of FDR's Administration (note the little NRA seal to the right of the dressing table). We can only guess at the occasion that has prompted this young mother to pay such careful attention to her gown and coiffure. A pretty woman, she seems to have modeled her style on some of the movie stars of the day—performers like Miriam Hopkins and Constance Bennett—a fact that cannot have escaped the attention of the *Post*'s readers when this cover appeared.

Whatever the circumstances, the woman's daughter, on her way to bed, is clearly not happy about being excluded from the events that are about to unfold, but Rockwell leaves to our imagination whether she is staring at her mother in disgust or gazing in admiration. The device of placing figures with their backs to the viewer is one that Rockwell has used frequently throughout his career. Sometimes, as in this instance, he creates a sense of ambiguity this way. At other times the pose leaves no doubt as to what we could see if the figure were facing us.

This painting is elegantly composed, the profile of the young woman's head against the mirror being especially effective. Note too that the *Post*'s editors have allowed Rockwell to bring the mirror up to the top of the page, eclipsing part of the logo, thus making a much stronger cover.

The Milkman and the Young Couple

MARCH 9, 1935

ONE OF THE INCIDENTAL PLEASURES of Rockwell's paintings derives from their small, documentary touches—details that sometimes manage to conjure up an entire era. How many of us remember, for example, that milkmen often carried flashlights when they delivered their wares? When Rockwell painted this cover he was merely trying to be true to life in portraying this milkman. In retrospect, however, the flashlight stands for a whole vanished life-style. In a time when we buy our milk in cardboard cartons plucked from the refrigerated shelves of supermarkets, we have no milkmen to stop on the way home from parties.

In its own quiet way this cover deals with class distinctions—a subject we do not generally associate with Rockwell's art. The tradesman, forced to rise before dawn to earn his living, seems faintly disapproving of the young couple who can afford to spend the night on the town. Rockwell does not pass judgment, however. He simply records the scene with his usual impassive accuracy.

No background is needed for this composition. Faces, clothes and postures tell us all we need to know.

The Interview

BACK IN THE MID-THIRTIES, when this cover was painted, interest in Hollywood was at its height, and the Hollywood press corps was almost as large as those that covered news events in New York and Washington. Movie stars were expected to dispense words of wisdom everywhere they went and were likely to be questioned by reporters on every subject from the latest Paris hats to the Ethiopian question. Some stars looked on all this as an invasion of their privacy, but others welcomed the attention and turned the celebrity interview into a minor art form.

The elegantly clad young lady who is conducting this informal press conference seems to belong to the latter group. She knows exactly the right pose to stike for the benefit of her public. She knows how to roll her eyes thoughtfully before answering even the most inane question. She understands that as a star she has certain responsibilities, and she is determined to fulfill them to the best of her ability.

The gentlemen of the press lean toward her. They do not want to miss a single word, but their earnest attitude suggests more than that. Confronted with a star, these hardened newsmen are fans like everyone else. They crowd as close as they can, basking in her glamour, inhaling her fragrance.

Rockwell captures the scene perfectly and imbues it with a gentle irony.

Barbershop Quartet

SEPTEMBER 26, 1936

FOR ROCKWELL, NOSTALGIA HAS ALWAYS BEEN a valid sentiment, and he has never been shy of exploiting its hold on the general public. When he painted this cover he was recalling an era that was already almost half a century in the past. That era may not have been quite as innocent and uncomplicated as he chose to portray it, but he convinces us of its reality by making the four singers seem so real. We can almost hear their voices as they harmonize some old favorite—"Down by the Old Mill Stream" perhaps—and this in turn evokes for us the clatter of horse-drawn buses and wagons on the cobbled streets outside the barbershop.

The fact that he works from live models and photographs of real people is an important feature of Rockwell's art. The authenticity of his character studies gives authority to the worlds he has chosen to evoke, whether he is casting an ironic glance at the contemporary scene or looking at the past through rose-colored glasses.

All Buttoned Up

MOTION PICTURES FREQUENTLY MAKE USE of what is known as the reaction shot. Instead of showing us every bit of action, movie-makers know that it is sometimes more dramatic to show the effect that an incident has on an observer, whether disinterested or otherwise. In this *Post* cover Norman Rockwell employed the same general principle very successfully.

We do not see the faces of the young lovers, we do not hear the sweet nothings that he is whispering in her ear, but we do see the reaction that the couple provokes on the features of a rather prim-looking gentleman attempting to lose himself in some inspirational work.

Many things combine to inform us of the old gentleman's prudishness: the way his hands grasp his book and his cane, the fact that his dog wears a coat. Everything about him contrasts with the casual affection of the lovers. The old gentleman belongs to the past—both in reality and in Rockwell's art. *Post* readers would not encounter many more of these frock-coated puritans. For the artist, as for the world, the future lay with the young man and woman on the other bench.

Missing the Dance

JANUARY 23, 1937

ROCKWELL RECORDS HERE ONE of the tragedies of adolescence —missing the big dance because of illness. What makes this cover work so well is the economy with which he evokes the scene. Rockwell is a splendid technician and, like any top-flight illustrator, knows both what elements are essential to any composition and which ones should be eliminated. Here he deliberately gives us the bare minimum. Except for the bedside table in the foreground, the image seems to fade at the edges. This has the effect of isolating the unfortunate girl in her misery. Rockwell paints her not as a clinical observer would see her but, rather, as she sees herself in this situation.

It is this ability to get inside the characters he paints—and to translate their feelings into pigment on canvas—that is the mark of Rockwell's mature work. It is the gift that makes him such a fine storyteller and such a sympathetic observer of the human comedy.

The Final Curtain

JUNE 12, 1937

WHEN ROCKWELL PAINTED THIS COVER, vaudeville was already on its last legs. For more than a decade performers like Dolores and Eddie, Gaiety Dance Team, had been forced to play second fiddle to the movies, and with every year of the Depression their situation had become worse. By 1937 only a few large theaters, such as Radio City Music Hall, were providing their patrons with live shows as a supplement to the motion pictures that were their mainstay. The sad truth is that not too many people would pay to see Dolores and Eddie when they could see Fred Astaire and Ginger Rogers (whom the unfortunate vaude-villians seem to be doing their best to resemble.)

This is a very well-conceived cover, with the symmetrically posed figures and the oversized theatrical trunk being used to create a strong abstract design against the page. The pathos of the situation is conveyed by the expressions on the performers' faces. They realize that their life of five shows a day, of split weeks in Seattle and Spokane, is over, but Rockwell gives them a certain dignity. Even in their dejection he allows them to have the grace and suppleness of dancers.

The Artist

OCTOBER 8, 1938

THERE MUST HAVE BEEN TIMES when even Norman Rockwell's seemingly bottomless well of invention ran dry, and here he amusingly illustrates just such a situation. The artist is presumably a self-caricature. He is caught at that dreadful moment, faced with a canvas that is terrifyingly blank except for the familiar *Post* logo. Abandoned sketches have been cast aside, and his palette lies untended on the floor.

Did Rockwell feel, one can't help wondering, that the cover artist's work was taken a little too much for granted? Month after month, year after year, Rockwell and his peers came up with new ideas and fresh variations on old themes, but the efforts involved probably never even occurred to the millions of readers who picked up the *Post* every week. It's easy to believe that he got a special pleasure out of this particular composition.

Freedom of Speech

1943

TOO OLD TO GET INTO WORLD WAR II, Norman Rockwell decided to help the war effort in the best way he could. The result was the famous "Four Freedoms," completed in 1943. The paintings were inspired by remarks that Franklin Delano Roosevelt had made in a Presidential address to Congress two years earlier. Roosevelt had spoken of his ideals for the future of the world and condensed these into the basic notions of freedom of speech, freedom of worship, freedom from want and freedom from fear.

Rather than try to project these ideals onto the world as a whole, Rockwell showed them as he saw them applying to the United States. In "Freedom of Speech" he decided to illustrate grass-roots democracy at work in a small New England community. At the annual town meeting a young blue-collar worker stands up to state his views on some matter that is clearly of great importance to him. Rockwell's viewpoint—that anyone and everyone can have a voice in American politics—is conveyed directly and succinctly.

The artist makes the young speaker an heroic figure, his battered work jacket worn as a badge of honor. The townsfolk who surround him listen to him with respect. The composition is strong and simple, with the young man's head silhouetted against what appears to be a blackboard. It may be that this meeting is taking place in the very schoolroom where he learned the principles that have now brought him to his feet.

Rejected at first in Washington, "The Four Freedoms" was bought and published as an inside supplement by the *Post*. Much later the Office of War Infomation reproduced them by the hundreds of thousands—even dropping copies into the European war front.

"Freedom of Speech" was a favorite of Rockwell's. When the curator of American painting at the Metropolitan Museum of Art in New York wanted a Rockwell painting for their collection, Rockwell chose to make and send a smaller version of "Freedom of Speech."

Freedom of Worship

1943

ROCKWELL'S VERSIONS OF "The Four Freedoms" were subsequently exhibited all over the country during World War II and were instrumental in selling hundreds of thousands of dollars' worth of War Bonds. It is, in fact, difficult to judge these paintings by normal standards because they belong as much to the realm of patriotism as to the world of art.

The one thing that all four canvases have in common is the fact that they convey their messages with a minimum of fuss. To represent "Freedom of Worship" Rockwell simply painted people of different faiths joined in the act of prayer. Heads, seen in profile, and hands fill the canvas. The color scheme is almost monochromatic, and there is very little depth of image, so that the composition reads almost like a photograph of a sculpted relief.

To emphasize the point he is making, Rockwell included the legend "Each according to the dictates of his own conscience," but this seems a trifle unnecessary, since the image speaks eloquently for itself.

EACH ACCORDING TO THE DICTATES OF HIS OWN CONSCIENCE

NORMAN ROCKWELL

Freedom from Want

1943

IN THIS, THE THIRD OF "The Four Freedoms" Rockwell used every visual device available to him—from the happy expression on the faces of the gathered family to the sunlight gleaming on the china—to convey the full meaning of "Freedom from Want." The occasion appears to be Thanksgiving, in itself a celebration of this particular freedom, and a grandmother places a turkey, that most American of birds, on a white tablecloth before her children and grandchildren. Her husband, an approving look on his face, waits to demonstrate his skill with the carving knife.

Again, Rockwell is at pains to make it clear that he sees the United States as the home of "The Four Freedoms." The fact that this canvas was painted at a time when rationing was in force must have made it all the more effective.

Freedom from Fear

1943

Freedom from Fear IS THE MOST EFFECTIVE and affecting of Rockwell's "Four Freedoms." A husband and wife are shown watching their sleeping children. It is the most ordinary of scenes, and it is this fact that makes the painting so convincing. Rockwell seems to be saying here that our freedom is most valuable when we can take it for granted.

In this painting Rockwell captures one of those everyday domestic moments that he handles so well and makes it the medium through which he transmits a universal message. It belongs to the mainstream of his art, but the circumstances under which it was conceived give it a special meaning.

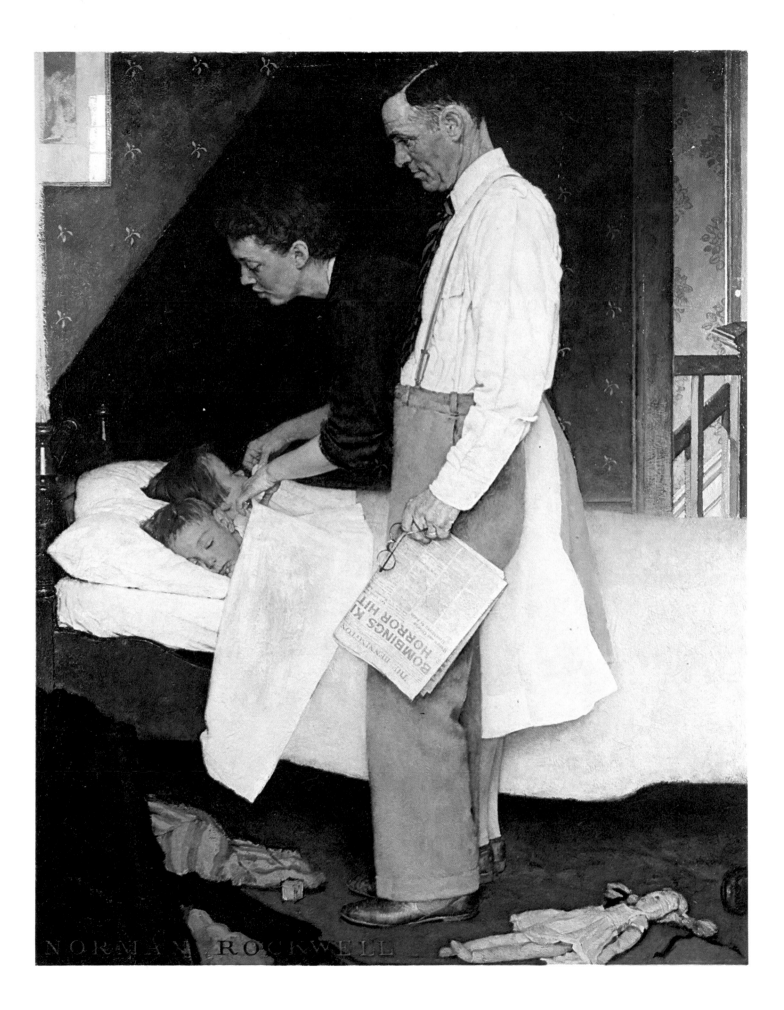

BOMBINGS KI
HORROR HIT

THE BENNINGTON

NORMAN ROCKWELL

The Tattooist

MARCH 4, 1944

The Tattooist IS ONE OF NORMAN ROCKWELL'S best known and most humorous wartime cover paintings. The joke is an obvious one—the kind you might expect to find furnishing the basis for a one-panel newspaper cartoon—but Rockwell gives the two figures enough personality to make this more than just a simple sight gag. The sailor (modeled by Rockwell's friend and fellow illustrator, Mead Schaeffer) is a bruiser of a man, with a face that has been through naval battles, storms at sea and barroom brawls from San Diego to Singapore. He is rather like the kind of character that was played by Wallace Beery in some of the war movies of the period. His jacket, draped over his knees, gives us a couple of clues to his personal attributes. The ribbons pinned there attest to his bravery. The comb projecting from a pocket hints that he may not be totally free of vanity. It is amusing to picture this battered sea dog courting Sadie, Rosietta, Ming Fu, Mimi, Olga, Sing Lee and Betty.

Rockwell has always enjoyed portraying artists at work, and he treats the tattooist with no less respect than he would any other artist. His calling may not be an exalted one, but Rockwell shows him as a model of concentration, a craftsman proud of his skill, busy on his living canvas.

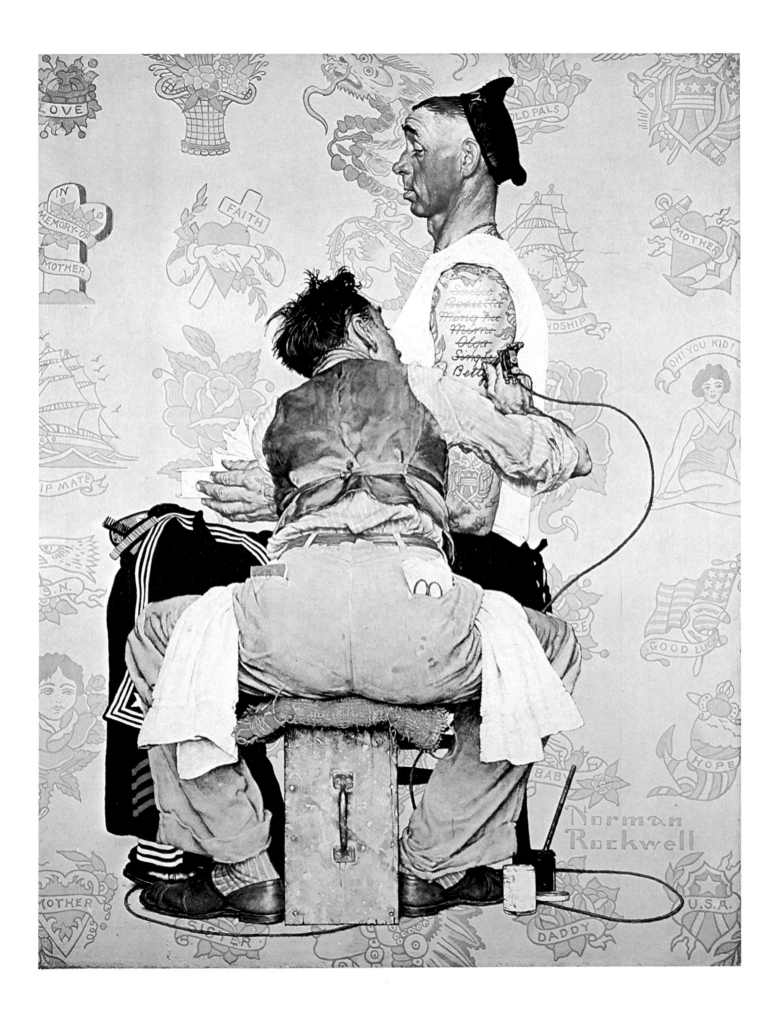

Homecoming GI

MAY 26, 1945

IN WHAT WAS TO BECOME ONE of his most celebrated *Post* covers, Rockwell painted a young, redheaded GI returning home safely from the war. All the predictable elements for a successful tear-jerker are present. The aproned mother waits with open arms. Father and sisters gasp with delight. The kid brother and the dog rush to greet the returning hero, while neighbors, who have their own sons in the service, look on. The girl next door, who has blossomed during his absence, waits shyly to be noticed.

It is a painting packed solid with sentiment, a fact that can easily be justified by the time in which it was painted. It is all the more effective because, rather than set his homecoming in some comfortable suburban environment, Rockwell chose to locate it in a big-city tenement area. This might be the Lower East Side of Manhattan or the South Side of Boston, and the feeling of closeness that we associate with such neighborhoods lends an extra emotional kick to the painting.

Rockwell portrays the subject faithfully, without attempting to glamorize it in any way.

War News

1945

NORMAN ROCKWELL SEEMS TO HAVE been a lifelong connoisseur of humble dining establishments. Again and again he has lavished his affection on diners, truck stops, coffeeshops, malt shops, soda fountains and cafeterias. Each of these he has re-created on canvas with such a feeling for the realities of the place that you can almost smell the bacon frying on the griddle. His naturalism goes beyond the careful observation of the physical objects that make up such an environment—the cheap dinnerware, the vinyl seats of the bar stools, the functional tiled floor—to an understanding of its ambiance.

This is true of all his interiors. We always sense the human presences and practical contingencies that have shaped them. They exist in time as well as space.

In the present example we know that we are being shown real people in a real setting. There is an intimacy about this group that is totally convincing. We understand the relationship of the three men without having to be told a word of dialogue. We are presented with just enough of the interior itself to know exactly what kind of place it is. From the information we are given it is easy for us to conjure up the rest of the room, other customers, even the kind of neighborhood it might be situated in. As in most of his best work, Rockwell uses one apparently insignificant tableau to evoke an entire way of life.

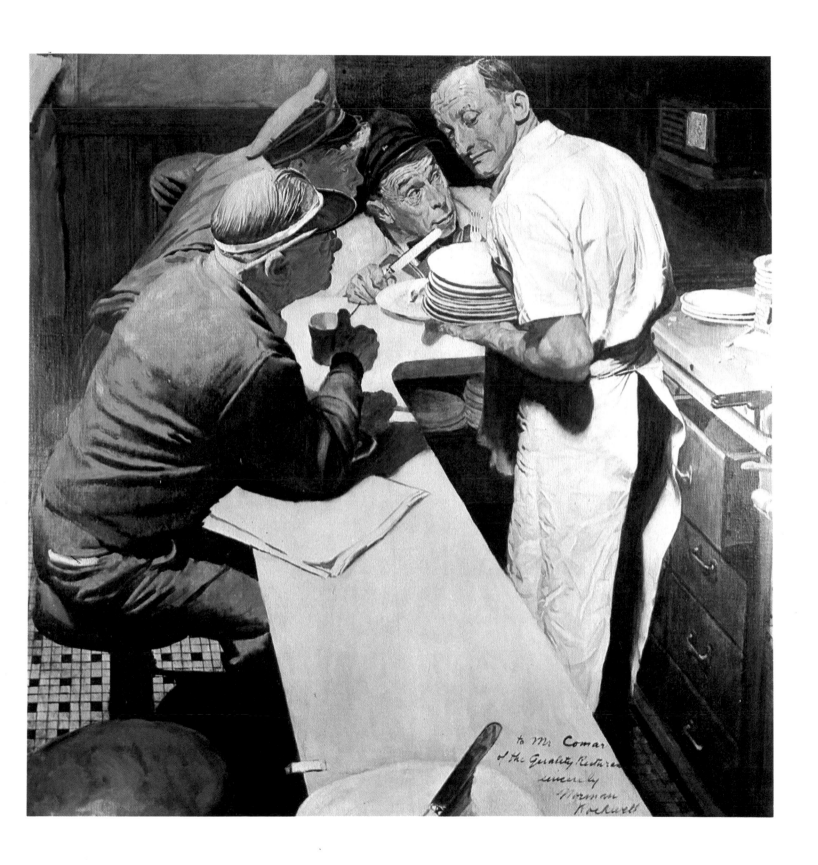

to Mr Coman
of the Quality Restaurant
Sincerely
Norman
Rockwell

Thanksgiving

IT HAS BEEN ONE OF NORMAN ROCKWELL's great blessings as an illustrator that he has never been afraid to present the obvious. Lesser artists sometimes shy away from it, fearful that it will make their work seem banal. Rockwell—perfectly capable of producing novel ideas when the occasion demands—knows that the obvious can often be very powerful, realizing that the subtlety with which an idea is presented can have more to do with its impact than the cleverness of the idea itself.

For the first Thanksgiving after the end of World War II, Rockwell took an obvious subject—the veteran back in familiar surroundings—and used all his powers of sympathetic observation to bring it to life.

Often we are able to guess at the dialogue that might accompany an incident that he has painted. In this instance the emotions that have welled up in both mother and son take them beyond words. Just being together in the same room is all the communication that is needed. The painting is still moving today. At the time it first appeared its impact must have been tremendous.

Fixing A Flat

AUGUST 3, 1946

ONCE AGAIN ROCKWELL DEMONSTRATES that his vision of rural America is not always idyllic. We can assume that the two young ladies, toiling to change a wheel on their heavily laden station wagon, are off in search of picturesque scenes. Instead they find themselves stranded beside a rustic eyesore. The weather is threatening, and the hillbilly who studies them from his tottering porch clearly has little regard for the romantic qualities of this mountain landscape.

As always, Rockwell concentrates on the situation. This may be something that he stumbled on in his travels, or it may have come straight out of his head; but, whatever the case, having decided on his subject, he follows through and takes it to its logical conclusion. The treatment is naturalistic, but he never loses sight of the fact that he is contrasting two very different life-styles and that the effectiveness of his painting depends on clearly displaying symbols of those life-styles.

norman
rockwell

The Outing

AUGUST 30, 1947

The Outing IS A CLASSIC EXAMPLE of a "before and after" painting that takes as its subject matter a situation that anyone can identify with. In the upper panel a family is setting out for a day trip to the country. Everyone is in high spirits. Father, chomping on a freshly lit cigar, sits erect at the wheel of a sedan that is old enough to have been used for many such expeditions. His wife is beside him, their youngest daughter in her lap. Another daughter blows out bubble gum, and the family's two sons lean from open windows, one of them making derisive faces at the occupants of a late-model car that is just coming into the picture. Even the family dog is full of anticipation.

In the lower panel the same family is returning home at the end of the day, spent and exhausted. Father, chewing on an unlit stub, is slumped over the wheel. His wife is asleep, and the children can barely keep their eyes open. Only the grandmother, stoic on the back seat, remains unchanged. She has been on too many outings to allow herself the luxury of an emotional buildup, so she alone has escaped the subsequent letdown.

What makes these panels so effective is the fact that Rockwell manages to tell us so much about the people on this expedition. The vintage of the car and the number of children tells us that this is a family that has known hard times. No one in this car takes luxuries for granted, and so a day trip to Bennington Lake is an important event in their lives. This knowledge engages our sympathy and makes the contrast between the two panels moving rather than just amusing.

The Gossips

MARCH 6, 1948

IT CANNOT BE STATED TOO OFTEN that Norman Rockwell is a master of pictorial narrative, and in this *tour de force* he drives the point home by telling a story about the telling—and retelling—of a story. His subject is nothing less than the spoken word—specifically the transmission of gossip—something that would seem to fall entirely outside the province of the graphic artist. He succeeds in giving us everything we need to know by means of an almost cinematic sequence of character studies. We never learn the substance of the calumnies that are being passed from neighbor to neighbor, but the reactions of the fifteen individuals involved in this cycle are more than enough to convey his message.

Each of these characters—from the born gossip who starts the ball rolling to the loudmouth in the derby hat and the unfortunate victim of the whole episode—is a recognizable type who might be found in any neighborhood.

Almost thirty years later another artist borrowed this basic idea to compose a cover that adorned telephone directories in many parts of the United States. To make it clear that this was intended as a tribute to Rockwell, he was included as one of the characters in the sequence.

Four Seasons Calendar:
Grandpa and Me Going Fishing

SPRING 1948

ROCKWELL HAS PRODUCED MANY CALENDARS, and this one is typical, taking the form of a set of variations on one of his favorite themes—the contrast of age and youth. A grandfather is shown enjoying the *al fresco* delights of the four seasons along with his grandson and the boy's pet dog. It is impossible to say whether it is the boy or the old man who gets the most out of the idyllic settings Rockwell places them in. In a century that has not treated old people kindly, Rockwell, from the very beginning of his career, has always depicted them with great respect, showing them as capable of enjoying life as much as anyone else. Rockwell always stands for continuity. It's easy to imagine that the boys and girls who appeared in his early works are the grandparents of his later paintings, and, while the artist always managed to move with the times, each successive generation is shown enjoying many of the same pleasures as those that went before.

Four Seasons Calendar:
Grandpa and Me in Summer

SUMMER 1948

ROCKWELL WAS BORN IN NEW YORK CITY, on the Upper West Side, but is on record as saying that he always preferred the countryside to anything that Manhattan had to offer. As a boy he always looked forward to summer because it meant that he would, for a while, be able to escape the brick-and-asphalt environment that imprisoned him for the balance of the year. Summer was a time when the entire Rockwell family left the city for a long, rustic vacation.

With this in mind we can assume that Rockwell had little difficulty in transporting himself back to those idyllic days when he painted this picture. The picture captures, without fuss, long, languid afternoons spent on grassy slopes breathing in the scents of nature and dozing beneath a sky alive with butterflies.

Four Seasons Calendar: Grandpa and Me in Fall

FALL 1948

IN THIS COMPOSITION ROCKWELL SHOWS the boy wrapped up in youth's eternal fascination with fire, while his grandfather responds to the waning of the year by striking a philosophical pose as the geese head south.

Fall, Rockwell seems to say, separates youth from age more than any other season.

Four Seasons Calendar:
Grandpa and Me Ice-skating

WINTER 1948

IT IS CRUCIAL TO THIS LITTLE SUITE of seasonal paintings that Rockwell depicts Grandpa at his most vigorous in a setting of ice and snow. Nothing could be better calculated to show the youthfulness of his spirit. On a day that should send him scurrying to the fireside with aching bones, he dazzles his grandson with his skill on skates.

The atmosphere of the other paintings in this group is tranquil. This one is full of movement. In the others the grandfather is lost in contemplation. In this one he is allowed a triumphant smile as he glances down at the perfect figure eight he has executed.

Game Called Because of Rain

APRIL 23, 1949

When Norman Rockwell paints sporting events he seldom deals with the excitement of the athletic contest itself. In this instance he selected the exact moment at which a ball game is brought to a premature conclusion by inclement weather. The delight of the Brooklyn manager, who can be glimpsed behind the umpires assembled in the foreground, is prompted by the fact that his opponents, the Pittsburgh Pirates, are ahead by one run, but his score will not go into the record books unless Brooklyn gets another opportunity to bat in the bottom half of the inning. The Pittsburgh fielders are already in position, waiting for the Dodger batters to come to the plate. The rain is on the Dodgers' side.

By selecting an eye level at about the height of the pitcher's mound, Rockwell transforms the three umpires into a monumental, though faintly comical, group and at the same time focuses attention on the sky, from which the rain is beginning to fall.

The painting now hangs in the Baseball Hall of Fame in Cooperstown, New York. The Brooklyn manager is the former catcher Clyde Sukeforth; the Pittsburgh manager is Billy Meyer. Dixie Walker is at bottom left. And the umpires, left to right, are Larry Gaetz, Beans Reardon and Lou Jorda.

Traffic Conditions

JULY 9, 1949

IN THIS EXAMPLE FROM THE LATE Forties, Rockwell took the format that was demanded by *Post* covers during that period and packed it with colorful characters. There are no fewer than twenty figures in this paintings—relatively unusual in his cover art—not counting the creature that is the center of all attention. Each figure—the artist and his model, the cyclist, the music teacher, her approaching student and his haughty mother, down to the toddler in his sagging diapers—is beautifully characterized. The liveliness of the work is ironic, given its subject.

A truck is blocking a narrow alleyway, its progress made impossible by a truculent bulldog. The incident gives Rockwell the opportunity to evoke lovingly a slightly run-down neighborhood and the people who inhabit it.

Shuffleton's Barbershop

APRIL 29, 1950

IF WE WERE TO MAKE A LIST OF Rockwell's half-dozen finest works, "Shuffleton's Barbershop" would have to be included. He succeeded here, perhaps more than in any other work, in blending the demands of illustration with the concerns of the the fine artist. This painting was made for a *Post* cover and obeys all the rules of storytelling that we associate with his cover art. But Rockwell might just as well have painted it for his own pleasure, and it could hang on a gallery wall without seeming in any way out of place.

Never has Rockwell lavished more affection on an interior. We do not doubt for one moment that we are being given a glimpse of a real barbershop. (The artist, in fact, used dozens of photographs to ensure the accuracy of every detail.) But this scene is more than just a documentary record of a charming American backwater. Rockwell imbues it with a tremendous warmth. We sense his deep involvement with the subject matter.

By placing the window frame and the cracked pane of glass in the foreground, Rockwell was able to create an illusion of depth that greatly enhances his treatment of the scene. The lighting too is beautifully considered. In fact, every element of this painting seems to have been weighed with great care.

The Plumbers

JUNE 2, 1951

WHEN ROCKWELL PAINTED THIS cover he—and the magazine's editors—must have been working on the assumption that most of the *Post*'s readers would find it easier to identify with this pair of plumbers than with the owner of the boudoir in which they find themselves. The owner is absent, of course, but a beribboned Pekinese acts as her surrogate, casting a baleful eye on the proceedings while seeking protection from them near the wastebasket. The setting tells us a good deal about the room's usual occupant. Note in particular the invitations wedged into the frame of the oval mirror (which, in its Gallic ornateness, gives us a clue to the aspirations of the woman whose face it is its duty to reflect). Clearly, this room belongs to woman who likes to be seen in society, something of a big wheel in her chosen circle.

As for the intruders, they are a well-realized pair of comic characters, a little reminiscent of Laurel and Hardy. No words are needed to communicate their opinion of this environment. The idea of placing likable characters in unlikely surroundings is one that Rockwell used over and over again. Because of his inventiveness and his careful attention to character and detail, he seldom failed to make it work.

Saying Grace

NOVEMBER 24, 1951

Saying Grace MAY BE THE BEST known of all Norman Rockwell's *Post* covers, and it is not hard to see why it has remained such a great favorite. The idea of the small boy and his grandmother thanking God for their food in a seedy railroad-station cafeteria was custom-made for Rockwell's particular skills, and he did not fail to make the most of the opportunity.

The environment is superbly evoked. It is essential that it should be if the incident is to touch the viewer in the way it is intended to. The detail of the Juniper Street Horn and Hardart cafeteria in Philadelphia (the railroad station out the window was added) is wonderful, and we should note, in particular, the still-life arrangement in the left foreground. The cold coffee in the clumsy restaurant-ware cup and the soggy cigarette ends lying in the saucer are somehow exactly what was needed to set off the simple piety of the old woman and the child. Nothing could be more down to earth than cold coffee and soggy cigarette butts. (The boy at the table with his back to the window is Rockwell's oldest son, Jerry.)

Much of Rockwell's early work was carefully planned to read as a powerful design against the page on which it was intended to be seen. In this painting, as in many later examples, Rockwell used instead a "snapshot" approach. The figures cut off at the both sides of the canvas emphasize this. Rockwell was borrowing from the art of the photographer to give the impression that this was a real incident that he happened to capture at just the right moment. He leaves us with the feeling that we are witnesses to the event.

Walking to Church

APRIL 4, 1953

ROCKWELL HIMSELF HAS CRITICIZED this painting, saying that it
was a mistake to treat the churchbound family as caricatures
since it weakens the impact of an otherwise naturalistic painting. Certainly most of the interest resides in the background,
which is superbly rendered in an idiom reminiscent of the work
of the Dutch realists of the seventeenth century. Rockwell gives
us here a scrupulously honest portrait of a down-at-heel
neighborhood in one of our older Northern cities. There is
garbage on the streets, and you can almost smell yesterday's
pork chops in the dining roon of the Silver Slipper Grill. The
adventures of Steve Canyon and Little Orphan Annie are waiting to be read on front-door steps. Windows are open to admit
the mild, spring air, while birds are scattered by the bell that
clangs in the nearby church steeple. The weathered façades of
the buildings—each several generations old—are lovingly
rendered by the artist, who does not exclude from his painting,
however, the television antennae that have sprouted on the
roofs at a much more recent date.

This is Rockwell's tribute to the kind of neighborhood that
one of his great contemporaries, Edward Hopper, loved to
paint. Rockwell's approach is far more traditional than
Hopper's—he paints in a style that was current long before
these buildings were erected—but the picture is nonetheless
touching for that.

Girl at the Mirror

MARCH 6, 1954

ROCKWELL HAS SAID THAT HE feels he has been more successful at capturing the world of the small boy than that of the young girl. As a general rule, this has been true, but here is an instance where an exception must be made. In painting this girl on the brink of womanhood, studying herself in a mirror, a movie star's portrait resting on her knees, Rockwell has been completely successful in capturing the poignancy of the moment.

The picture has the immediacy of a snapshot, but this is tempered by the mellowness of oil paint on canvas. It is charged with symbolism—the doll cast aside tells us that that phase of the girl's life is almost over—yet this does not interfere with the naturalism of the overall treatment.

This is a subject that Rockwell might have tackled at almost any point in his career. We can be thankful that he painted it when his creative powers and sense of judgment were at their peak.

Breaking Home Ties

SEPTEMBER 25, 1954

Breaking Home Ties IS ONE OF NORMAN ROCKWELL'S finest paintings, an instance of his special gifts and decades of experience meeting in an ideal subject. Father and son sit on the running board of an ancient, battered truck beside the tracks of a rural railroad station. The son, dressed in his best suit, with a crisp, white shirt and a necktie that seems a little too gaudy, waits eagerly for the train that will carry him to college. The father, dressed in blue coveralls—he has the face and hands of a man who has spent his life in the fields, exposed to the elements—stares off into space, presumably contemplating the passage of time and the changes that his son's departure will bring to his life. The family's collie rests its chin on the boy's knee. The boy holds lunch carefully wrapped by his mother, who—perhaps because of the sadness of the occasion—has not come to see him off. The father holds two hats. His own is a practical, wide-brimmed number designed to shield him from sun and rain. His son's is a snappy new Stetson decorated with a colored band.

This is a thoughtful and controlled treatment of a subject that could easily have seemed maudlin. Both figures command our respect, and every detail is just right, down to the markers in the boy's textbooks, which tell us that, eager to continue his education, he has already begun his schoolwork.

A classic twentieth-century illustration.

The Critic

APRIL 16, 1955

IN THIS PAINTING FOR A 1955 *Post* COVER Rockwell plays a variation on the time-honored theme of paintings coming to life. An earnest young artist (Norman Rockwell's oldest son, Jerry, is the model) uses a magnifying glass to study the brushwork used for the locket on the bosom of a buxom young woman (posed by Mary, Rockwell's second wife) who appears to belong to the school of Rubens. Lost in this detail, he does not notice the coquettish smile and wide-eyed amusement that his act has provoked. Nor does he see the perturbed expressions on the faces of three bearded observers who reside on an adjacent canvas of the school of Frans Hals.

This painting begs the question: Was Rockwell making a wry point in this work? Was he warning young artists against the danger of paying too much attention to detail at the expense of the whole work?

Marriage License

JUNE 11, 1955

THERE CAN BE LITTLE DOUBT THAT this is one of Rockwell's finest works. The idea behind it is simple enough: The artist contrasts the young couple applying for a marriage license with the elderly clerk who has seen it all a thousand times before. But the scene is evoked with such affection that it becomes suffused with complex resonances.

The old clerk occupies an office that, like him, seems to belong to the past. It contains rows of dusty volumes and an ornate potbellied stove. Paint is peeling from the dingy walls and cigarette butts are scattered on the floor. But the tall sash window lets in the early-summer light, which falls on the young couple, bathing them in its glow and causing them to stand out from their surroundings. Their concentration on the task at hand is such that the surroundings have no meaning for them anyway. In this composition the play of darkness and light is used both to create the architecture of the painting and to produce an emotional effect on the viewer.

Everything about this painting seems just right. Artists are notoriously critical of their own work, but in this instance it is impossible to think that Rockwell cannot have been satisfied with the result of his labors.

Discovering Santa

DECEMBER 29, 1956

IF CHARLES DICKENS WAS THE literary master of the Christmas story, surely Norman Rockwell holds the equivalent position among illustrators. No one has rung more variations on the theme than he has. He has given us everything from traditional Santa Claus subjects to documentary treatment of Chicago's Union Station during the Christmas rush.

As his career progressed, it became more and more imperative for him to find new ways of dealing with Christmas. In 1940 he tried something rather original, painting a young boy on a subway train spotting an exhausted department-store Santa on his way home. A glimmer of realization is apparent in the boy's eyes, but the illusion is not completely shattered. We are permitted to assume that he still believes in Santa, even though he recognizes that the man he saw at the store was not the real thing.

In 1956 Rockwell took this idea one stage further. In a cover that appeared four days after Christmas, he showed another young boy—he seems to be about seven years old—exploring his father's bottom drawer, where he finds a Santa suit put away in mothballs for the following year. This time disillusion is complete.

New Man on the Team

MARCH 2, 1957

SINCE ROCKWELL IS, BY CHOICE, a New Englander, it's safe to assume that he is a Red Sox fan, so it was very natural for him to choose the Boston locker room for this spring-training cover. All eyes are on the rookie prospect who has just arrived in camp—all eyes but those of the great Ted Williams, who has, perhaps, seen this all too many times before to allow for much display of curiosity.

Rockwell uses the limited space of the locker room to create a mild sense of claustrophobia that helps us empathize with the young hopeful, who must feel a trifle overwhelmed to find himself in the presence of these heroes who, until now, were little more than pictures on bubble-gum cards.

Clearly, for Rockwell the ritual of spring training is a symbol of new hopes. Perhaps this year Ted Williams will lead the Sox to a pennant; perhaps the newcomer will get his first taste of the major leagues. Rockwell knows very well baseball is something that millions of Americans can identify with, and he exploits its folklore to the full.

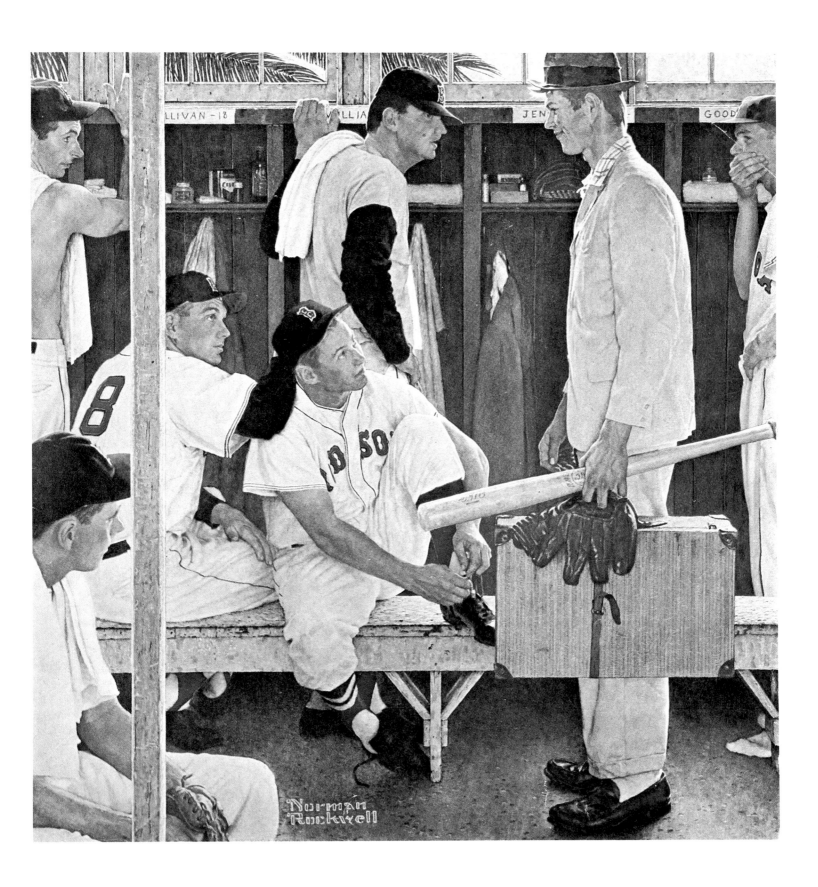

After the Prom

MAY 25, 1957

NORMAN ROCKWELL, LIKE ALL GREAT illustrators, is a master storyteller. He knows how to create characters, how to set a scene, how to give us the circumstances of a person's life with a few well-chosen details. The book illustrator, of course, has to work with characters created in advance by a writer. Rockwell has successfully illustrated many books, but he is at his best when—as is the case with his *Post* covers—he is free to invent a situation and characters from scratch. It is his gift that he is able to plant an entire story in our mind with a single image. In *After the Prom* he gives us the happy ending, and we are able to reconstruct for ourselves the events that led up to it. We can imagine how the evening began. We can even imagine the anxieties of the preceding weeks. We can picture the prom itself with a band in shawl-lapeled jackets doing its best to reproduce the latest hits of Elvis Presley and Pat Boone. We can conjure up the moment when the lights were lowered for the last waltz.

The notion of putting the young couple—the boy in his white tuxedo, the girl with her spectacular corsage—in a truck stop is a brilliant piece of invention. There is one enigma, though, that everyone must solve to his own satisfaction. The boy is clearly the son of the truck stop's owner—their features are almost identical—but is the girl a very special date, or did the boy take his own sister to the prom? Only Norman Rockwell knows for sure.

Checkup

SEPTEMBER 7, 1957

THERE ARE FEW ASPECTS OF GROWING up that Norman Rockwell has not painted at one time or another. The prestige of losing a tooth was something he captured convincingly in this 1957 *Post* cover.

The girl in the center of the composition may have already experienced the ecstasy that her friend is now enjoying, but the other observer, off to the left, is the picture of envy. She cannot wait to acquire the same badge of maturity.

Since a detailed setting would have done nothing to add to the effectiveness of this subject, Rockwell simply places the three figures against a neutral background. This does not mean, however, that he fails to pay attention to naturalistic details. In fact, details become all the more important in so simple a composition. His concern with naturalism can be seen by looking closely at the girls' shoes. Each girl is wearing sneakers, but each pair is laced in a different way.

Before the Shot

MARCH 15, 1958

IT IS EASY TO SEE THAT, had he not been a gifted artist, Norman Rockwell might well have become a successful writer or director for films or television. Situation comedy has been one of the most popular genres in both these mediums, and no one has a better knack for inventing comic situations than Rockwell. The scene he painted for the March 15, 1958, edition of the *Post* might have run into censorship problems from the Motion Picture Production Code, but otherwise it would work perfectly in a movie. The boy, about to receive his shot, takes advantage of the fact that the doctor's back is turned to satisfy himself that the doctor's credentials are in order. As usual in Rockwell's work, the single image suggests a whole sequence of events. We know what has gone before and what will come after.

Another skill that Rockwell has in common with filmmakers is the ability to create an authentic setting for each incident. In this case the setting is simple enough, but every detail is just right. All of us have been in rooms like this, and we know that the artist has taken care to make it convincing.

Weighing In

JUNE 28, 1958

FOR THIS *Post* COVER Rockwell relied on the simple drama of the event and his own sure sense of composition. There are only three elements in the picture: the jockey—Eddie Arcaro—the track steward and the scale on which Arcaro is being weighed. Rockwell makes much of the contrast in size between Arcaro and the steward, emphasizing this by having the steward hunched over, as he reads the scale, so that we feel he would literally tower over the jockey if he would only straighten up.

The composition is almost monumental in concept, but the artist has lightened it by making the most of the bright colors of the racing silks, the mud spattered on Arcaro's white riding pants, the stripes of the steward's shirt and other such details.

"Weighing In" shows a routine race-track event but one that is nonetheless filled with tension—a fact that is evident in the expressions of the two men. It is typical of Rockwell that he chose to portray this small, private drama rather than the very public spectacle of the race itself.

The Runaway

SEPTEMBER 20, 1958

ROCKWELL CONTRASTED THE WORLDS of childhood fantasy and adult authority on many occasions but never more effectively than in this 1958 *Post* cover. The fact that the state trooper, like the short-order cook behind the counter, is clearly in sympathy with the boy's dream of a life on the open road does not diminish from this since the contrast is established in visual terms. The cop's broad shoulders, uniform and sidearm are set off against the boy's slender physique, white tee shirt and pathetic travel kit.

Although Rockwell has dealt sympathetically with all the ages of man, his deepest and most spontaneous sympathies have always been with the world of the child. The child's imagination knows no bounds, and it is this to which Rockwell seems to respond. He does not shrink from dealing with the responsibilities of adulthood, but, in Rockwell's universe, the child is never far away. In this instance the cop and the cook have no difficulty placing themselves in the boy's position.

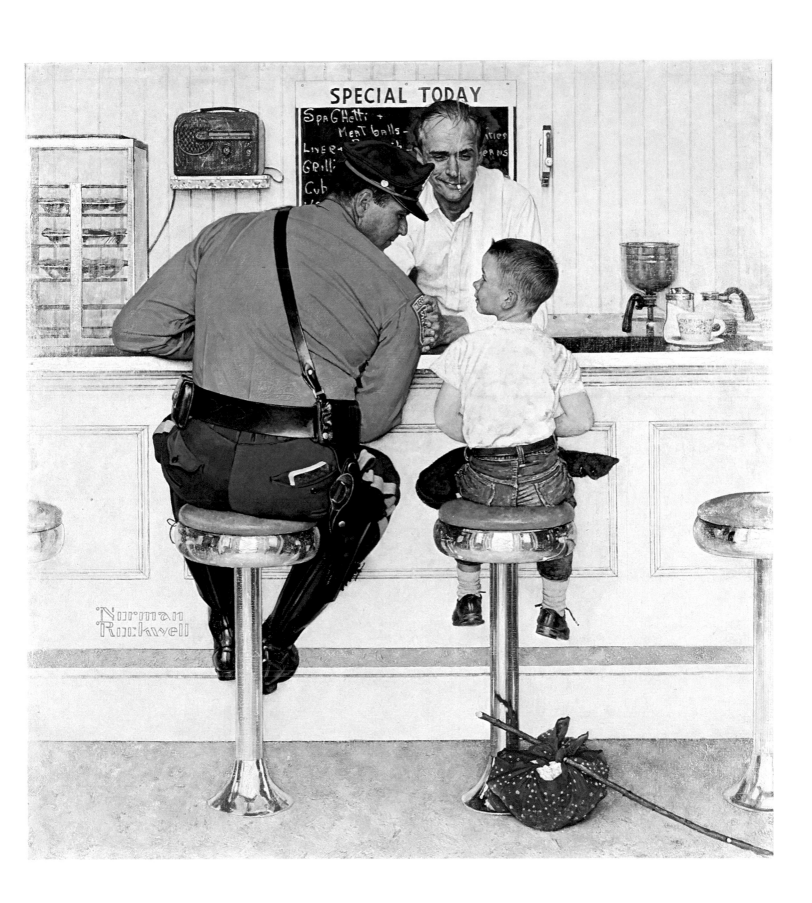

Before and After

NOVEMBER 8, 1958

ELECTION DAY IS ONE OF THOSE recurring subjects that Rockwell was called on to illustrate again and again. He has given us married couples fighting over their respective candidates and citizens still unsure as to which lever to pull as they enter the voting booth. In 1958 he zeroed in on an actual politician for a change. This man—apparently a candidate for some local office—is caught in the moment of defeat, his hopes as dead as the cigar that dangles from his fingers. Supporters are filing from the room, leaving the candidate alone with his thoughts. Judging from information scribbled on a pad that has fallen to the floor, his state of shock may derive not so much from the fact of defeat as from its magnitude.

Rockwell has painted portraits of a number of real-life politicians—from FDR to Richard Nixon—often giving these portraits an heroic turn. This unheroic representation of an exhausted, imaginary candidate, however, seems truer to Rockwell's vision of the world.

The Holdout

FEBRUARY 14, 1959

AT FIRST GLANCE THIS SEEMS to be a profoundly male-chauvinist painting—on a par with jokes about women drivers—but this is only because we expect conventional attitudes from a man of Rockwell's generation. The debris on the table and the floor tells us that the jury has been in session for many hours and the lone female juror is clearly the reason for the length of its deliberations. Is she a holdout from sheer feminine cussedness —are the eleven good men and true the victims of her native "irrationality"—or is the artist asking us to identify with her strong-minded independence, her ability to think for herself and view the facts of the case under consideration from a different perspective?

As so often, Rockwell asks us to make up our own minds, and a consensus of people viewing this picture would probably add up to a hung jury.

Easter Morning

MAY 16, 1959

THE HEAD OF THE HOUSEHOLD does his best to become invisible, but Rockwell's brush misses nothing. The argument is over, and soon the backslider will be able to enjoy the Sunday sports pages in peace, but first he must go through this final ritual embarrassment.

There are many ways in which this subject could have been treated, but, as usual, Rockwell picks exactly the key moment —right down to capturing the son's envious glance.

It might be observed in passing that Rockwell's art, through the years, has provided us with a remarkable record of trends in American interior decoration. Here we are into the Scandinavian Modern period, and Rockwell uses the shape of the spindly-legged chair cleverly to center his composition. It may be of interest to note also that the view through the window is in fact the view from Rockwell's studio.

A Family Tree

IN THIS SYMBOLIC FAMILY TREE Norman Rockwell tried to suggest something of the complexity of the American heritage, including Yankees and Confederates, yeomen and buccaneers, preachers (note Rockwell as preacher) and pioneers, fair-skinned and dark. This is the American heritage as most Americans choose to picture it, a genealogy that finds room for pirates as well as puritans, for aristocrats—note the coat of arms alongside the Spanish beauty—as well as commoners.

It is interesting that Rockwell—a New Englander by adoption—chose to portray the birth of the New World not at Plymouth Rock but on an isolated Southern shore, off which a privateer has launched an attack upon a treasure galleon.

a Family Tree by norman rockwell

Marriage Counselor

Early 1960s

ALTHOUGH NORMAN ROCKWELL TENDS to avoid extreme situations in his art, he does not attempt to present a world that is devoid of conflict. Many of his best works derive their energy from the differences of opinion that erupt in everyday life. In particular, Rockwell has never suggested that married life is a bed of roses. Domestic squabbles and disappointments have long been one of his stocks in trade. Seldom, however, has he given us cause to think that his marriage partners were in danger of being driven to consult with a marriage counselor.

The couple who find themselves in this counselor's waiting room seem so young that it is impossible for us to feel that their problems are too advanced to be solved. We can tell from their clothes that they are taking this visit very seriously. His pose, with arms stiffly folded, suggests that he is doing his best to remain unmoved. Her sidelong glance signals that she may be a little more flexible. We are encouraged to think, in fact, that if the counselor leaves them in this waiting room for long enough they might well resolve their differences without his intervention.

The composition is interesting and rather unusual. Half of the painting is taken up by the office door, which, in its blankness, seems to symbolize the unknown territory they are about to enter.

Triple Self-portrait

FEBRUARY 13, 1960

PERHAPS THE MOST INTERESTING ASPECT of this cleverly conceived self-portrait is the fact that the artist has chosen to give us a glimpse inside his head as well as multiple images of the face he shows the world. Pinned to his canvas are reproductions of paintings by four acknowledged masters. There are self-portraits by Dürer, Rembrandt and Van Gogh, and there is a post-cubist head by Picasso. That Dürer and Rembrandt are sources of inspiration to Rockwell will come as a surprise to no one, but some people may be a little nonplussed to find the expressionistic work of Van Gogh and the still more radical vision of Picasso sharing space with these more academic masterpieces.

The fact is that, despite the evidence of his work, Rockwell's taste is extremely catholic. Photographs of Rockwell's home and studio show a number of modern works hanging on his walls, and, in 1923, as the result of a stay in Paris, he had a brief experimental period of his own during which he did very little commercial work. The fact that he abandoned this experimental approach does not mean that he lost interest in the idioms of the twentieth century. Rather he decided to return to what he did best, a happy decision for all of us, but the symbolic inclusion of Picasso's work in this self-portrait tells us that his curiosity about modern art remained very much alive.

The University Club

AUGUST 27, 1960

IT'S WELL KNOWN THAT ALFRED HITCHCOCK likes to make token appearances in each of his movies, and audiences greet his arrival on screen with enthusiastic applause. It would have been impossible for Norman Rockwell to insert himself, like Whistler's butterfly, into each of his compositions, but occasionally he does make an unbilled appearance, as in this 1960 *Post* cover.

Rockwell can be glimpsed in the bottom left-hand corner of this painting, turning his head toward the two characters who are the focus of interest. He shares the curiosity—perhaps we should say wistfulness—of the old men in business suits who watch the same scene from the somber confines of New York's University Club.

A sailor is trying to pick up a pert little blonde in a neat red dress, and the situation evidently stirs memories in everyone's mind. For all the worldly distinction of the men within the club, we cannot doubt that there is not one of them who would not gladly be blackballed for the chance to take the place of the sailor out on the street.

Solitaire

AUGUST 19, 1950

ROCKWELL'S EYE FOR significant detail has seldom been more effectively employed than in this study of a travelling salesman passing away a lonely night on the road. The garish necktie on the back of the chair tells us about the man's professional manner, the shabby room tells us about his economic circumstances, and the glimpse we are given of the hotel sign—through the open window—evokes a whole urban landscape.

We can guess that, when making his sales pitch or at home with his friends, this man is given to tall tales and expansive gestures, but Rockwell unerringly captures the reality of his existence. Although the artist remains as sympathetic to his subject as ever, this painting is infused with a sense of melancholy which is rare in Rockwell's work.

The Golden Rule

APRIL 1, 1961

THIS PAINTING CAN BE TAKEN as a statement of Norman Rockwell's credo. To illustrate the saying "Do unto others as you would have them do unto you," he crowded his canvas with a symbolic catalogue of the family of man. Christians and Hindus, Muslims and Jews, Buddhists and Shintoists stand shoulder to shoulder in a hieratic composition that draws its strength from its solemnity.

Although not unique in Rockwell's work, this kind of painting is certainly atypical. Usually his work is designed to be seen to maximum effect on the printed page. In this instance we can imagine that the composition might have succeeded just as well—perhaps even better—if it had been executed as a mural.

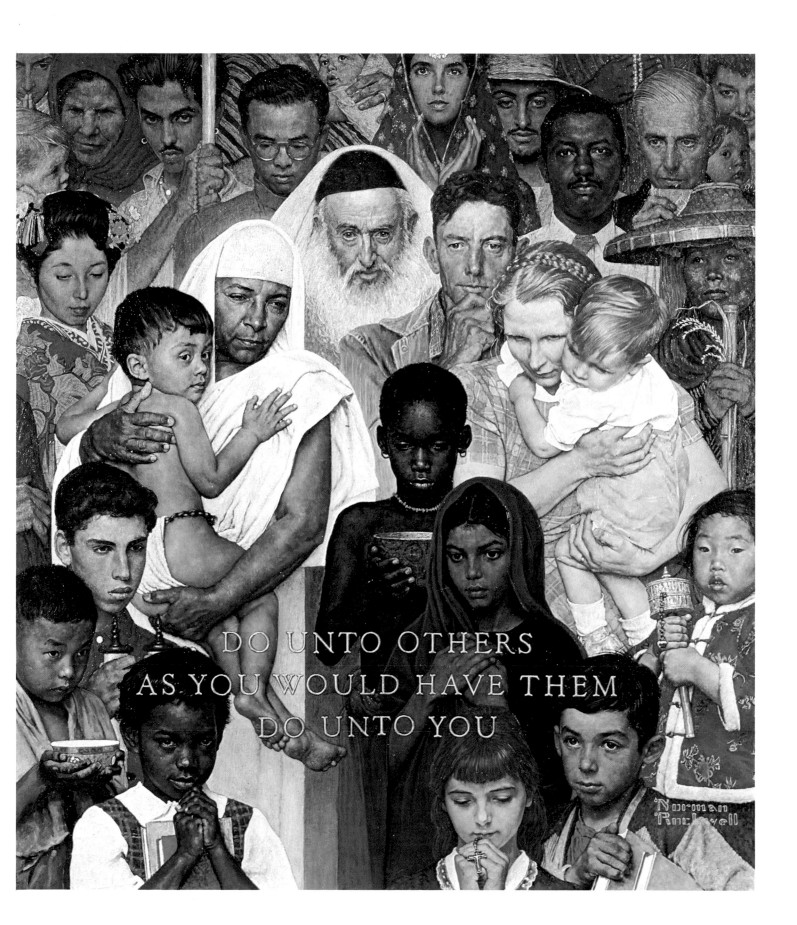

The Connoisseur

IT WOULD BE EASY ENOUGH, at first glance, to assume that Rockwell's primary intent in this *Post* cover was to make fun of contemporary art, and perhaps this is the case. The fact is, however, that this composition would have been just as funny—perhaps funnier—if the painting the man was contemplating was a well-known work by Norman Rockwell, *Shuffleton's Barber Shop*, for example. The bad imitation of Jackson Pollock's style is not intrinsically humorous, any more than a bad imitation of Rockwell's style would have been.

It is the relationship of the man to the canvas he is confronting that is funny. Judging by his dapper clothing and his self-assured pose, we can reasonably assume that he sees himself as a person of some discernment—yet we cannot imagine that he has any concept of what the artist has put himself through to produce this painting, whether it is good or bad. Rockwell is poking fun at people who set themselves up in judgment of others.

The Problem We All Live With

JANUARY 14, 1964

MANY PEOPLE WERE RATHER SURPRISED when this Norman Rockwell painting appeared in *Look* magazine. Rockwell was not a person the public associated with controversy, and the question of school integration—which is the subject of this work—was one of the most inflammatory issues of the day. Why, then, had he chosen to tackle it?

We must recognize, of course, that Rockwell is a commercial artist and often works on assignment, so the idea for this painting probably originated with the editors of *Look* rather than with the artist himself. At the same time, Rockwell is free to refuse assignments if he finds them unsympathetic, or if he feels he cannot make a good job of them, so we can assume that he did not embark on this project without having thought about it a good deal beforehand.

Rockwell's work shows him to be a natural egalitarian and a man who respects the dignity of every citizen, however humble. Given this, it was in fact very logical for the editors of *Look* to make him their choice to cover this confrontation. Rockwell's sympathy is entirely with the neatly dressed black girl, her situation made all the more poignant by the anonymity of the U.S. marshals assigned to protect her.

A Time for Greatness

JULY 14, 1964

NORMAN ROCKWELL BEGAN HIS CAREER at a time when the illustrator reigned supreme. Newsreels and photo-journalism were in their infancy; television was decades away. By the time he came to portray John F. Kennedy receiving the acclamation of the Democratic Party's National Convention for *Look* magazine the situation had changed radically. An event such as this was now covered by every imaginable kind of medium, and the public, bombarded with literally millions of images, was actually able to experience the event in the home as it happened.

In his portrayal of the occasion Rockwell fell back on the tried-and-true methods of his trade, counting on them to provide him with something that could not be achieved by any other means. He created a careful, studied composition, using the standards of half a dozen states to frame the President-to-be caught in an heroic pose. Rockwell's competitors, the photographers, are shown jockeying for position down among the delegates on the floor. By contrast, Rockwell was able to choose for himself a viewpoint high above the heads of the crowd.

Instead of trying to compete with the spontaneity of photo-journalism, he gives us a symbolic record of the event.

Spring Flowers

1969

NORMAN ROCKWELL IS, ABOVE ALL, a master of the character study. When we think of his art we think first of the way he portrays faces and hands, the skill with which he captures thoughts and emotions in expressions and poses. It should be remarked, then, that this charming still life, published in *McCall's,* is rather unusual in Rockwell's output because it does not include a single human figure.

This is not to say, however, that it does not include a human presence. The shoes, the gardening gloves, the beribboned hat on the potting-shed wall, the way the flowers and branches have been arranged in the basket on the comfortable-looking old chair—all these things tell us something about the woman who inhabits this environment. The tame-seeming bird perched in the doorway gives us another clue to her character.

Technically, then, this is a still life, but in a sense it is a portrait—a portrait of a woman who stays in touch with nature through the medium of her garden.

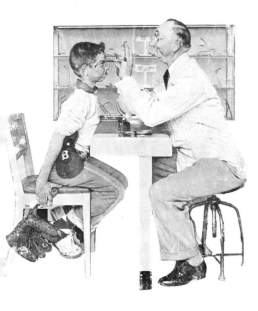

EYE EXAMINATION
(May 19, 1956)

THE FACTS OF LIFE
(July 14, 1951)

THE LETTERMAN
(November 19, 1938)

NORMAN ROCKWELL is a superb popular artist. It is his skill at manipulating shared symbols and sentiments that has made his work live in our collective imagination.

Rockwell painted his first *Post* cover almost a decade after Picasso painted *Les Demoiselles d'Avignon,* but we hardly need to be reminded of this to recognize that Rockwell is also a profoundly conservative artist—by no stretch of the imagination could he be thought of as aesthetically adventurous. But this does not mean that he has been unresponsive to his times. On the contrary, he has in his way been as sensitive as a barometer.

When one turns to a popular artist like Norman Rockwell, it is easy to suppose that every nuance is immediately available to the casual viewer because the language is so familiar. This is an illusion. The conventions of Rockwell's common sense realism allow all of us to feel at home in his world—this is his basic strength—but, within those conventions, Rockwell has discovered many new inflections and permutations.

In his work, Rockwell seldom travelled far from home, but he never ceased to explore. Discovering an unfamiliar corner of Vermont may not be as spectacular as climbing some previously unconquered peak in the Himalayas, but it has its own merits and brings its own rewards.

Illustrations continued on following pages . . .

BOOKWORM
(August 14, 1926)

HOMECOMING
(December 25, 1948)

ESCAPE TO ADVENTURE
(June 7, 1924)

SODA JERK
(August 22, 1953)

DAYDREAMS
(November 4, 1922)

DISCIPLINARY ACTION
(May 23, 1953)

GRANDPA'S PRESENT
(January 25, 1936)

GARY COOPER AS THE TEXAN
(May 24, 1930)

NEW YORK CENTRAL DINER
(December 7, 1946)

SHIP AHOY
(August 19, 1922)

WAR HERO
(October 13, 1945)

FIREFIGHTERS
(March 28, 1931)

THE WINDOW WASHER
(September 17, 1960)

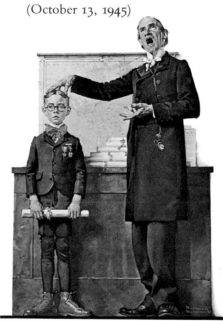

SCHOLAR
(June 26, 1926)

ON LEAVE
(September 15, 1945)

THE DUGOUT
(September 4, 1948)

YOUNG ARTIST
(June 4, 1927)

THE CHAMP
(April 29, 1922)

OUT OF A SCRAPE
(September 14, 1935)

CHRISTMAS EVE
(December 27, 1947)

MEASURE OF LOVE
(March 10, 1923)

PROM DRESS
(March 19, 1949)

AT TEA TIME
(January 12, 1929)

PIANO TUNER
(January 11, 1947)

HARD NIGHT AT WORK
(November 8, 1947)

SANTA'S HELPERS
(December 2, 1922)

TICKET AGENT
(April 24, 1937)